I Protest!

Other poetry anthologies published by Ginninderra Press
First Refuge (edited by Ann Nadge)
Wild (edited by Joan Fenney)
Mountain Secrets (edited by Joan Fenney)

I Protest!
Poems of Dissent

Selected by Stephen Matthews

I Protest! Poems of Dissent
ISBN 978 1 76041 906 6
Copyright © poems indivdual contributors 2020
Copyright © this collection Ginninderra Press 2020
Cover image: Justin Martin from Pixabay

First published 2020 by
Ginninderra Press
PO Box 3461 Port Adelaide 5015 Australia
www.ginninderrapress.com.au

Contents

Introduction	Stephen Matthews	12
Numbers count	Nance Cookson	13
Just saying	Louise Nicholas	14
The Believer is a Non-believer	Jill Gower	15
Silent protest	Linda Albertson	16
Summer Villanelle	Roslyn McFarland	17
The PM before the last PM…	Linda Wells	18
Emergency Planning	Jacqui Merckenschlager	19
Let Them Eat Cake	M L Grace	20
yesterday's news	jenni nixon	21
'The Interview'	Doug Gregory	22
A True Conservative	John Egan	23
Clancy of the Underflow…	John Watson	24
God's Own	Mark Miller	25
Wake Up and Smell the Humans	Sean Crawley	26
A Kind of Paralysis	William Cotter	27
Political Correctness	Karen Throssell	28
Marionettes in Exile	Michelle Gaddes	29
Quiet Australians	Rosemary Winderlich	30
Cyclical Changes	Helene Castles	31
Midden, Grass Point	Anne Morgan	32
Towards Healing: A Memo to God	Fran Graham	33
Kali Speaks	Janette Dadd	34
To the islands	Adèle Ogiér Jones	35
Shame the Devil	Mary Jones	36
Broken Record	Allan Lake	37
hurrah	Jordie Albiston	38
Advance Australia	John Bartlett	39
upsizing	Kathleen Bleakley	40
The road of lost dreams	Geoff Neville	41

Rhyme and Reason	Ann Simic	42
dust bowl days	Kevin Gillam	43
The Plasto BottleO Virus	Millicent Jones	44
The Plastic Age	Pippa Kay	45
One of the Lucky Country's Crowd	Hazel Hall	46
eat your porridge	Jacqueline Buswell	47
Good Karma Pudding	Joe Dolce	48
Reiterate	Jen Gibson	49
Some Sort of Reason	Danny Gardner	50
Disconnect	Michael Keating	51
It's Only	Geoff Lucas	52
The Grey-headed Flying Fox	Cassandra O'Loughlin	53
Intergalactic Tourism	Indrani Perera	54
Advocating the Earth	Adrian Rogers	55
Backwater	Brenda Saunders	56
Haiku	Garth Alperstein	57
…the affairs of men…	Janet Upcher	58
Ad Break	Melinda Jane	59
The Front Moves Closer	Derek Baines	60
The Burning of the Great Statue	Jane Carmody	61
Burning Times	Jocelyn Munro	62
A Prayer From the Inferno	Mark Cornell	63
Lungs	PS Cottier	64
Cloudy Skies, No Rain	Catharine Steinberg	65
In Silence	Kathryn Fry	66
If…	Bernadette Anderson	67
No fireworks	Dawn Colsey	68
A Kinder World	Margaret Clark	69
The heat's on	Brendan Doyle	70
A Tree's Despair	Kristin Martin	71
Prometheus	Carolyn Masel	72
Choking	Decima Wraxall	73

A Privileged Life	Brenda Eldridge	74
The Final Stand	Ian McFarlane	75
Industrial Revolution	Maureen Mendelowitz	76
Action to stop Climate Change!	Robyn Cairns	77
Difficult Endeavours	Judi Hearn	78
the ashes of ignorance	Myra King	79
Sonnet from the heart	Jack Oats	80
Black Stump	Tim Metcalf	81
Fly the Rag	James Finlay	82
All Too Readily	Rodney Williams	83
Illegal Becoming Legal	Stuart Rees	84
A Lament	Barbara Fisher	85
Collateral Damage	Dianne Kennedy	86
Hitchhiker	Sue Cook	87
No one cares	Margitta Acker	88
Too Many Birthdays	Gordon McPherson	89
The Unread File	Marilyn Revill	90
Unbalanced	Betty McKenzie-Tubb	91
Ars Gratia Artis	Gillian Telford	92
Give Me Olive Trees	Tracey-Anne Forbes	93
I will not be cremated!	David Harris	94
Small town	Pip Griffin	95
The Question	Ken Setter	96
Free Speech?	Carolyn Cordon	97
A bull's eye view	Jude Aquilina	98
I Remember It Well	Alice Shore	99
Papercuts	Natalie D-Napoleon	100
From the shadows of Weston Street	Joan Fenney	101
Legalities	Anne Landers	102
Molestation	Margo Poirier	103
Home Sweet Home	Melissa Bruce	104
No Game	Martin Christmas	105

A Lovers' Protest	Mary Pomfret	106
No Codpieces…	Gina Mercer	107
Women Are Reclaiming Our Lives	Gabrielle Journey Jones	108
Women who dare	Avril Bradley	109
Commercial-in-confidence	Anne Collins	110
Protest Poets in Prison	Thérèse Corfiatis	111
What Goes Around…	Mark d'Arbon	112
Dissent	Suzanne Edgar	113
I Will Protest	M. Fermanis-Winward	114
Best Protest	Roger Furphy	115
Stain	Virgil Goncalves	116
Suspense	Libby Goodsir	117
Defiance	Geoff Graetz	118
Credo	Graeme Hetherington	119
a poem with needles in it	Helga Jermy	120
Haiku	Judith E.P. Johnson	121
No need	Jayne Linke	122
Things	Jean McArthur	123
One Sheep	Colleen Moyne	124
Rage again	Liz Newton	125
The Seven (St)ages of Outrage	Julie Thorndyke	126
A question	Valerie Volk	127
The Unconquered	Wendell Watt	128
Last rites	Luke Whitington	129
Elephants on surfboards	Tony Steven Williams	130
Reclaiming the Square	Paul Williamson	131
Not Guilty	Jean Winter	132
Cosmic Eye	Adriana K Wood	133
The fall of Communism	Paul Cliff	134
Speaking of Borders	Jena Woodhouse	135
Frangipani in Barbwire	Donna Edwards	136
Dissent	Rose Helen Mitchell	137

Visitant	Philip Radmall	138
this city is gay and cool to me	Sandra Renew	139
'Some monks were born to smile'	Steve Tolbert	140
Into the fray with LBJ	Greg Tome	141
Of Birds and Poets	Maurice Whelan	142
rock-a-bye baby	Colleen Keating	143
Night of the Supermoon	Stephen Smithyman	144
The Passing of the Fly	Tony Fawcus	145
The Apostrophe's Lament	Maureen Mitson	146
Milk	Ros Schulz	147

The voice of protest, of warning, of appeal is never more needed than when the clamour of fife and drum, echoed by the press and too often by the pulpit, is bidding all men fall in and keep step and obey in silence the tyrannous word of command. Then, more than ever, it is the duty of the good citizen not to be silent.

– Charles Eliot Norton (1827–1908)

We must dare to think 'unthinkable' thoughts. We must learn to explore all the options and possibilities that confront us in a complex and rapidly changing world. We must learn to welcome and not to fear the voices of dissent. We must dare to think about 'unthinkable things' because when things become unthinkable, thinking stops and action becomes mindless.

– James William Fulbright (1905–1995)

Foreword

I Protest: Poems of Dissent was conceived in October 2019 when Brenda and I were in the Blue Mountains for the launch of *Mountain Secrets*. I had for some time wanted to publish a collection of poems with a political slant but hadn't been able to narrow down a focus for such a book. By coincidence, there were at the time mutterings from our benighted government about cracking down on dissent, with such ideas being mooted as stripping pensions from protesters. Also, one of the contributors to this anthology, Michele Fermanis-Winward, was at the time writing poems of protest about climate change.

Of course, at that time none of us knew that we were headed for a summer of calamitous bushfires (although even then smoke from early outbreaks was creeping into the Blue Mountains) and no one could have guessed that the fires would be followed by a virus that would confine us to our homes and commit us to an unfathomably uncertain future.

As the virus threat grew, I found myself putting off working on *I Protest*, wondering if the book would stand up in the face of the crisis. However, when I started reading and assessing the many poems we had received, it was clear that, although many of them inevitably addressed the bushfires, climate issues and political inertia that were at the front of most people's minds in late 2019 and early 2020, many also took a more general view, illustrating the importance of protest and dissent now and throughout history. Many poems also reflect how political and social activism can be an antidote to the despair that can accompany existential crises like global warming and (arguably not unconnected) new concerns like zoonotic viruses.

In these pages are to be found anger, anxiety, compassion, insight and sharp observation, expressed in the way that is the special gift of poets. There's humour too, to leaven the more serious poems.

Like our earlier poetry anthologies, *I Protest* demonstrates the Australia-wide breadth of talent in the ranks of poets who have been published by Ginninderra Press.

This is a collection to savour, to ponder and to celebrate.

Stephen Matthews

Numbers count

Numbers count
I've seen it happen
Voices too

I've heard it said

Standing firm
with your opinion

Speak out
Protest

Let them know
your blood is red.

Nance Cookson

Just saying

Dear Prime Minister,
There's no point
praying
if you're sitting
on your hands.

Louise Nicholas

The Believer is a Non-believer

I protest a political leader who turns a blind eye
to climate change. Maybe he believes that his prayers
to god will somehow resolve the issues. I'm angry that he
condemns the solidarity of our youth for their protests.
I am enraged by his arrogant smirks and glib words
'it's going to be a good summer for cricket' while
Australia burns around us. I protest his broken promises
and his lack of leadership. I object to dollars intended
for people with disabilities having been repurposed
for drought relief. I'm enraged by Adani and other coal
mines that threaten our health, water resources, forests
and farmland. I believe our indigenous Australians
should have more say regarding mining on their lands.
I protest politicians that believe refugees locked up
as prisoners offshore should be refused medical
treatment in Australia. I deplore our leader's errors
of judgement regarding our bushfires. His insistence
on shaking people's hands when they clearly reject him
and even worse, for not knowing that two people
had died in the fires on Kangaroo Island. I protest the
funding cuts to ABC, our national broadcasting station.
Perhaps if there is a god listening, we should ask him
to protect us from our politicians before our land,
our animals and our people are destroyed completely.

Jill Gower

Silent protest

His words sound like the shirt he's wearing –
psychedelic paisley with a 70s vernacular.
His beefy tone competes
with his prominent lisp,
sibilants hiss.

I stop listening.
Stare at the washing on the line.

So long.
Too long.

My head feels damp and heavy –
I retreat into a space
where I can wish for plain sentences, blowing
warm words towards me.

The washing hangs limp, it'll never dry today.

Linda Albertson

Summer Villanelle

(with apologies to Wendy Cope)

You're sure you know what you should do –
You smirk. You spin. You lie outright.
I think of nothing else but you.

It's hell to have a leader who
Deserts his nation and takes flight.
You believe you know what to do

'Cause you're arrogant through and through.
But as skies darken into night,
I start to feel contempt for you.

Climate action you do eschew.
Clutching coal like a troglodyte,
You're certain you know what to do.

With your dumb baseball cap askew,
You're nothing but a blatherskite.
I have an aversion to you.

You don't care. You haven't a clue.
But this I know, this much is right –
You have no vision that is true.
I absolutely can't stand you.

Roslyn McFarland

The PM before the last PM before this one

We stopped the boats
And dropped the totes
And hopped the potes
And scopped the groats

We axed the tax
And faxed the sax
And smacked the bax
And scrapped the wax

We screwed the gits and cashed the chits
We are fuckwits

Linda Wells

Emergency Planning

Now here's the thing, nowhere to go, nowhere really safe
no boundaries on a catastrophic day. The children cry out
to our leaders for meaningful climate policies
They cry out in anguish, in rage. They cry out
feeling more despair than they can bare.

And still he smiles, to comfort them, says they should
be in school, setting themselves up for a good job
Forget the slogans, the speeches, the marches, the sit-ins
ignore the greenies, send them back to their caves
forget their chants of fear and disaster, their chaos.

There's this then, he is caught in a time lag, won't change
These students don't believe him. They say
there are no jobs on a dead planet No life in a burnt forest
No water in a new dam. No joy while there's no action
You cannot avert their gaze from the real issues.

Don't talk to us of surpluses, or growing the economy
don't tell us to be quiet. Our teenage years should be
filled with hope, love, joy, a time to discover our true path
don't tell us to put aside our fears. It helps somehow
to come together and share our rage at your inaction!

Jacqui Merckenschlager

Let Them Eat Cake

How selfish are the citizens who doth protest
Their chosen prime leader taking flight
With his family over yuletide.
Everyone has entitlements and doubly so,
A man of such magnitude, who stood
And addressed a crowd…that booed.

They protest these people, who do not
Seem to comprehend, yet they themselves
Turn their backs to society with audacious
Propriety feeling absolutely entitled to
Party on and take a Christmas break…
I say oil the blade and let them eat cake.

M L Grace

yesterday's news

forests burn   skies on fire   33 deaths   3,000 homes lost
blackened sentinels on 12 million burnt hectares
greedy politicians make promises they won't keep
to reduce emissions can find no common ground
drought-hit farmers given loans   mining company mates
access free water   tax incentives they never need refund
fracking / drilling contaminates quality drinking water
strip-mining the seabed   the sludge destroys ecosystems
rising sea levels sink low-lying Pacific nations
Great Barrier Reef bleached white in warm acidic seas
overfishing   the ocean fish stocks fall   fish flap-flop
in dirt puddles on dry riverbeds   rainforests blaze
estimate wildfires kill *a billion mammals reptiles birds*
burrowing   crawly creatures   face imminent extinction
whales gobble plastic   their bloated bodies beach on sand
bats and birds no longer fly   drop dead from on high
the list goes on   air full of smoke and poison particles
flames finger ancient trees where koalas grasp the sky
PM delays plan to fly overseas promoting coal / gas exports
why in these burning times are fears and anger false?
ravings of inner-city loonies   bloody disgrace talk now
worldwide on Fridays   children take to the streets
Save Our Future   Fight Climate Change or Die Frying

                              jenni nixon

'The Interview'

The minister was asked ten questions
The first
He didn't want to answer
Skirting around the issue
The second he contradicted what
The opposition minister said yesterday
One of them…is a blatant liar
The third he answered
With a torrent of programmed
Well rehearsed standard lines and clichés
Which meant nothing
The fourth…he sounded ridiculous
Out of touch and condescending
The next and the next and the next
He combined all his expertise at evasion and trickery
And contempt for the people
Who put him in his job.
The remainder are a blur
As I fought to contain my fury at
Our parliamentarians
Keeping the truth
To themselves.

Doug Gregory

A True Conservative

He was greatly interested in Economics
and worshipped the Great God Market. Under his
government the rich did very well.

A career politician without vision,
he looked uncomfortable with those
not entirely North Shore, middle-class and white.

A true conservative who disdained unseemly
social change, the humane issues really bored
his suburban, mercenary, accountant's brain.

He enshrined the monarchy, Menzies and test cricket.
This prime minister casually admitted
his greatest achievement was just staying in power.

Through two American wars, imprisoned refugees,
his white blindfold views captured the certainty
of the 50s, though fifty years too late.

John Egan

Clancy of the Underflow Considers the Environment

Where is the vision splendid
Of the sunlit plains extended
And a million million solar panels spread?

John Watson

God's Own

On a morning of fraying mist, near the river's entrance
fishing boats are heading out, cutting lesions,
draping blood-orange lights over the water.

Along the bank the late, luminous moon
still shines down on the middens of abalone shells,
cigarette butts, rusting beer cans and tangled line.

Back from the strand, in the acacia and tea-trees,
beside the track to the dunes a blue wren skitters
from a broken deckchair to the litter of plastic bottles

and half-burnt fence posts. Now a jet ski
chainsaws the silence, smashing through waves,
splitting swell, after swell…

On the blue-bottled sand, amongst the tide's detritus
of sea-wrack and shredded balloons,
a punctured fuel can lies half buried.

In the distance, away from the backwash of diesel spume,
board-riders bob on the water like black buoys,
the sun is now blazing yellow, the morning new and clean…

in God's Own.

Mark Miller

Wake Up and Smell the Humans

Hey, are you thinking what I am thinking?
What everyone's thinking is wrong
That to keep ourselves going, we gotta keep growing
But there's only one planet we're on

Hey, are you shopping where I am shopping?
'Cause where everyone's shopping is wrong
That corporate super centre is killing my village
And that's where our money belongs

Hey, are you working like I am working?
And can't stop to question why
'Cause the roof over your head is owned by the bank
And ownership's based on a lie

Hey, are you thinking what I am thinking?
That nobody's thinking at all
And while the world never stops for us to get off
We continue to ignore the call

Wake up and smell the humans
The species you find everywhere
It's time we all stopped competing
Don't we teach our children to share?

Sean Crawley

A Kind of Paralysis

Bloated fish bottleneck our dying rivers.
Blackened tree stumps stand,
Bleak as tombstones in our landscapes.
A lump of coal,
Brandished like Arthur's Excalibur
Above the heads of our legislators,
Is pronounced 'good for humanity'.
Politicians obediently repeat 'Jobs and Growth'
And rusted on global warming deniers
Maintain greenies or left leaning chalkies
Have hoodwinked innocent, street marching students
And dismiss a teenaged girl,
Armed with nothing more than the truths of science,
As the victim of autism, manipulation or both.

Discomforted in our deckchairs,
We may scan the papers or the TV news,
Desperate to find some oasis,
Some sign of hope in the desert of our making.

Well may the children,
Well may the planet itself,
Rise up in revolt or dismay.

William Cotter

Political Correctness

Professional protesters – just out to have fun
It's part of the image, they're all the same ones

at every demo with their banners and flags
Hipsters with nose rings, abuse-shrieking hags

Up the workers! Down with wealth!
Free refugees (Oh, my heart melts)

Bleat about Climate, weep for the trees
Cry over koalas, scream about bees

Political correctness has got out of hand
Humourless wowsers who don't understand

for our system to work we must put profit first
which protects our great lifestyle and fattens the purse

of the men at the top of the corporate world
who ensure that the capitalist flag stays unfurled

And remember, you whingers, we have it all planned
Of course the earth's future will be safe in our hands…

Karen Throssell

Marionettes in Exile

They affixed a shackle this time,
the state – violent, whipping puppet master.
Your morale, so 'broken,' you say.
I prop you up with my grail of loud whispers,
throwing pieces of my skin at you to sustain.
You prop me up with perfect poetry
pouring into the vein of my heart, but,
desperate, appealing to the stoic gavel,
we are marionettes, falling over
each other every drawn-out day.
We look for the secure, free line –
it flails loosely inside the Palace of Justice.
And we cry to sleep – nightly –
under the chiselled curfews, while
I cradle your head to my breast,
tearing frantically at our strings.

Michelle Gaddes

Quiet Australians

Skewed balance…poor penalised
powerful rewarded for their power
powerless exploited.

Silence…almost
a few brave, lonely voices dissent.
Listen…can you hear the groans
the yearnings of the oppressed?

Quiet Australians
we trusted politicians to speak.
No more…we must bravely stand
or get what we deserve
make a choice…but…there is no choice
unless we use it, we forfeit our voice

Surely we can see the inhumanity
of those who misuse our voices
our silence?

Rosemary Winderlich

Cyclical Changes

Trolls have stalked the Minister for Injections.
Clowns are stripping naked on the greens.
Friends are made; we tally their affections.
Children seeing short, from watching screens.

The world has been entranced by the elections.
Heads of state and subjects, talking Trump,
aware there may be truths and wild deceptions,
the walls he builds, too high for folks to jump.

The spider crabs are gathered, having hurried
to moult their shells in shallows in the bay.
They're safe to humans, why should we be worried?
They're two months early, so the scientists say.

The Senate's busy fixing feuds and flaws.
A shopping trend, evolving globally,
leaves amateur *importers* free of laws.
Distributors declare the Shipping Free.

Helene Castles

Midden, Grass Point

Take this flake of chert in your right hand.
Study the scrapes in its crystalline smoothness.
Place your index finger in this depression;
your thumb in the depression beneath it.
Knuckle it. Scrape shellfish from this rock.
Apply heat. Relish the bounty
of this headland as it was in 1788
when William Bligh brought his goats
ashore to graze here.
You are entangled now with quantum traces
of this eolith's last user.
Feel her grief for the annihilation of her world.
And as Gaia burns,
quakes and shivers and drowns,
know that we may not be waving
but drowning in a toxic sediment
of post-truths.

Anne Morgan

Towards Healing: A Memo to God

Some of your most trusted machinery
has been seriously malfunctioning
due to faults in the integrity of the original material
and therefore its inability to do the job
for which it was originally ordained.
These apparent flaws seem to be widespread.
The reliability of the whole has now been
undermined by the failure of the parts
causing permanent injury to children
and parents alike and has even resulted
in a significant number of deaths.
Department heads have been slow to accept liability
and to recall and replace the rogue components.
We ask that you, as CEO of the organisation
resolved the crisis forthwith
and deliver us from evil.

Fran Graham

Kali Speaks

Enough
What you do is wrong.
You devour this Earth!
I will devour you!
In the dystopia of the flame her presence was all pervading
returning me to the dark void of a coal black abyss
of no time, no form – a place unknown.
No Earth for feet to feel I floated in a surreal scape
of silver-grey that stole away distance
questioning perception's gaze with soft illusion.
I arrive with power of breath
And transformation
Unleashing my wrath on civilisation.
I wept when the Black Goddess's landscape revealed her truth
wept in bewilderment of sureties removed
wept for a planet needing soft hand's healing
not the grasping, tearing, gouging,
violations of an anthropocentric view.
Weeping has its measure and listening its wealth.

Kali speaks
I will renew!

Janette Dadd

To the islands

We protest the threat of urban heat islands
no escaping the hell we find now created
no treasure islands of romance
floating remote in a dreamtime paradise
tropical exotica imagined in Defoe's famed tale.

Told of Pacific island solutions working
where others live imagined dream-states, forgetful
luscious living where sun greets calm ocean
overtones of holiday resorts, failing, far from
the torment and loss Boochani chronicles.

Complete isolation, disconnected from a world
beyond the road round the island cycled for fun
in Nauru long ago, working assignment,
glad to leave with odorous phosphate miners
as confinement cracked limits of psyche.

We protest those confined, silenced persons
beached, locked on islands not of their making
by rulers, parties to imprisonment of minds
of real people struggling, just a chance, no lawless
intent, one more breakdown Randolph Stow knew.

Adèle Ogiér Jones

Shame the Devil

Truth lies buried at the bottom of a mine.
naked, alone, and well and truly fracked.
She was abused by power, hidden and ignored.

Fact has lost ground to fiction and pretence,
history battles myth, and science falls,
all drowning in a rising tide of lies.

Knowledge is trumped by ignorant belief,
the only voices hailed as genuine
those of delusion or malevolence.

The devil plays truth, dare or promise,
always opts for promises, never keeps them,
meets straight questions with a crooked answer.

The only way to liberate the truth
is to dig deep into her hiding places,
and rescue her so she can set us free.

Mary Jones

Broken Record

Smoke is in the air (yes, feel free
to sing it). Temperatures rising
and I'm coaxing a body to dance
that would rather rest in peace.
This must be what it feels like
to be in this state of emergence
from stupor. Species pride: first
to foul an entire planet and space
around it. How good are *Homo
sapiens*? Not a question but answer
to be announced, post enquiry
of undetermined length and breath.
Homo erectus and other extinct
upgrade apes apparently got us
where we swelteringly are but
what down/upgrade gets us out
out of here. (Yes, go on, sing it.)

Allan Lake

hurrah

for what?   there are banners bunting chanting
cheers   & streamers & slogans line the street
from right up there to down here   the trumpets
trumpet & loveless letters litter the
air like confetti   a dog has a scratch

& the crowd starts to itch with concerns both
profound & petty   flyers & flags hang
like gurus from gallows   & soapboxes
shriek from street to street as the Commonwealth
law allows   pamphlets police a party

of people everywhere everywhere laud-
ing high praise   the whole of country the whole
of everyone commonly joined in this
day of days   celebrate! celebrate! now
but for what?   hip hip hooray   we forgot

Jordie Albiston

Advance Australia

the greatest country   another indigenous woman dies
in the world   in custody
for we are young and free   we need to protect children
                              from gender fluid ideology

we've boundless plains
to share   Reza Barati murdered
                              on Manus
we've golden soil and wealth dead cattle, dry paddocks,
                              a man in an Akubra
                              weeping
we're going to meet Kyoto 2   choking on smoke
at a canter   the habitat of the eastern
                              ground parrot is
                              being destroyed
talk to the real Australians 19-year-old mother,
                              took her life
                              because of robo-debt

                              Advance Australia Fair

John Bartlett

upsizing

would you like fries with that? no thanks
buying tissues boxes full
been weeping since john wayne galloped
back into our living rooms
gotta keep clearing them trees he said
that morning masses woke from long slumber
od-ed on piles of super processed creamy crispy donuts
when they woke john wayne was on tv
would you like fries with that? buying tissues boxes full
been weeping since the crowning of the new president
people bought loads of coke & toasted him
waved flags – stars & stripes
hung them on their front fences & cars
would you like fries with that? buying tissues boxes full
been weeping since i started picking up coke cans
from parks, gardens & creeks
in rainforests, on the beach & in the ocean
would you like fries with that? buying tissues boxes full
been weeping since they started building another mega store
there used to be a nursery there
we'd walk down come back with armfuls of plants
next time i'm asked *would you like fries with that?*
i'll say *no thanks i'll have seeds*

Kathleen Bleakley

The road of lost dreams

I see by the wayside a picture
Of where am I now, old mate
You sat by my side in campfire glow
Though I thought I was alone.
You help me when the booze
Went and let me down
I see a picture, old mate
And there's sadness in me heart
The ways of my people shackled
As Australians loses identity
And dignity is no more
I respected my elders
And proudly put pen to vote
I rode with Ned Kelly
Fought for justice to all
Downed my tools for a fair go
I sailed across the seas
Wearing khaki green
Now lord they tell me
I am in the wrong
I am Australia
From ball and chain
I am what I am
Please bring back
My country

Geoff Neville

Rhyme and Reason

Sonorous oboes reverberate deep speechless rage,
broken with the bees, tipping point ravaged. Agony.
Screams of dying creatures shatter our airless, thought-
less cauldron. Wrenching sobs, helpless horror.

Time will not quell rending hearts or bodies tense and
clenched on jagged tenterhooks of fear, fizzle, fury.
Calm deep breaths outflanked by blackest thoughts.
Guilt of survivor who smelt smoke, saw furious flames,

felt terror. Can sanity be saved while venting venom on
deniers parading dumb disdainful swagger while lives are
lost and risked? We chide ourselves for not roaring louder,
longer, to hammer home the risks beyond our grasp.

Stoop to change pain to powerful patience. Supplant the
impotence of turmoil and failure, to force action on those
who sit on money gifting it to grubby, groping Adani.

I spy two river mermaids, mother and child, basking in the
shallow Shoalhaven luring rain so mighty waters flow again:
buoyancy rises in unflinching resolve against extinction.

Ann Simic

dust bowl days

it was in April I believe,
on a Sunday. Frankie was

on the veranda, chewing
his 'bacco, spitting and

staring, staring into nothing.
'see how spotty that wheat is

out there?' my eyes take in
swaths of rippling stubble.

'well that short stuff shouldn't be
brindled like that.' 'Drought turns 18.'

that was the header of the
weekly rag. our eyes meet.

'these are dust bowl days.' a gob
of his spit folds in gravel

Kevin Gillam

The Plasto BottleO Virus

All day we traipsed the wretched waste
laced on the chafing saddle
embraced by blazing sizzling sun
that stole our precious water,
clean, sweet, water.
In times gone by you'd hear our cry
mustering in the desperate dry, crack
the whip, beat the flies, flipping dust from dusty
eyes, the water bag dead and souls that bled for
clean, sweet, water.
Now it's bottles, bottles everywhere, drink water, drink
using toxic PET we swig it down without a blink –
if you're riding on your bike, or heading off to school, at
the movies, by the beach, make sure your plastic bottle is
never out of reach.
You do not guess, care not a jot while sipping on the train,
when drinking at your office desk or jogging in the rain, of
processing this devil plague its transportation and disposal
effecting greenhouse gases, fire and waste – sucking dry our
clean, sweet, water.
I fear the carbon footprint is so far from your mind – but
just a single plastic bottle will help to wreck mankind.
So stop the rot, be rid the lot, turn on your tap with joy
and feel the bliss, the lover's kiss of
clean, sweet, water.

Millicent Jones

The Plastic Age

Heavy with eggs a turtle struggles up the beach
to dig a nest, where her eggs will incubate.
She doesn't hang around to watch
the slaughter as her soft-shelled hatchlings
dodge birds on their scramble to the sea.
Empty and hungry she swims away
to eat for the first time in months.
If she mistakes plastic for jellyfish she'll choke.

Her fat friend, the dugong, grazes on seagrass.
Every few years she calves, just one at a time.
Her mammary glands, like women's breasts
(which fooled lustful sailors who dreamed
of mermaids) will feed her calf for over a year.
But this doting mother can't hold her breath
like a turtle. If she's gets tangled in plastic
or nylon fishing line she'll drown.

Imagine a future when turtles and dugongs
are the shells and bones of antiquity.
Archaeologists will unearth our rubbish.
They'll call them victims of the plastic age.
How much plastic will it take
to suffocate our oceans?

Pippa Kay

One of the Lucky Country's Crowd

You're tagged like a cadaver. Then you're given
a show bag with disposable over-clothes:
zip-up space suit finished with a hoodie,
and shower cap of polypropylene.
Eyedrop bottle, sterile in its cover,
cannula comes plastic-wrapped as well.
Off you go to dreamland on a needle;
wake to find it's over. Half-hour lapsed.
Recovery with tea and packaged biscuits,
plastic case with sandwiches inside.
As you check out from this privileged position,
one of the lucky country's crowd,
muse on the dilemma we must face
now nations overseas won't take our waste.

Hazel Hall

eat your porridge

we who are comfortable
indeed injure and offend
with our motor cars, our excess of things
our ready water, hot and cold

our plastics that threaten to overcome
the fish in the oceans, our waking
in the morning and coming home at night
to turn on a dozen appliances

remember as a child being told
eat your food, there are millions starving
and wondering how you could help
by eating your porridge, your greens?

we should have found a solution then
and shared the porridge and greens
for we have grown fat
and uneasy in our comfort

Jacqueline Buswell

Good Karma Pudding

Ingrédients:
Bolivian yak milk.
Zen wine, warmed over burning ghee-brushed cow patty.
Free-range fairy penguin eggs.
Hydroponic Cordovan blood orange.
Organic vanilla bean pod, dried for 24 hours,
on a Venezuelan Socialist's roof tile.
Biodynamically grown Australian paperbark.
Cage-free echidna butter.

Méthode:
Preheat a solar-powered, or bicycle-pedal driven, pizza oven,
to lowest temperature. Combine penguin eggs, yak milk,
blood orange rind and vanilla pod, in a small prayer bowl.
Whisk, non-violently folding-in, yin with yang.
Sit on South American embroidered cushion, for three days.
Non-destructively brush both sides of paperbark pieces
with echidna butter, place into a hand-thrown stone bowl,
into the oven, facing away from the door,
(being mindful of feng shui.)
Meditate 30 minutes.
Ring a prayer bell.
Bake until custard is firm.

Servir:
Place on a bed of shaved glacial ice, if desired,
(although the goal is to be free from desire.)
Serves one small carbon-footprint-free village.

Joe Dolce

Reiterate

All the world's a slave to
dysentery of spirit:
across continents, fires burn and wars bugle
distraught skies funnel smoking furnaces
        of windy chaos

We are the Dispossessed and in
our helplessness may lie
        Salvation
        a rescue from the insignificant, absurd
rampage of Media's mad message

When trivialities Trump-ette as news
the meaningful's forgot:
        gentle creatures and plants wither
drone bombs and germs demolish…

While Nature's plenty perishes
revisioning our pain-filled, squinting eyes
can we wake up?

Jen Gibson

Some Sort of Reason

We, apparently, have some sort of reason,
to dam the rivers and rape the forests,
to dig up the ground and concrete the grass,
to cage all the wild animals and fish out the seas,
to pollute the air and poison the water,
to reconcile our actions in half-truths to each other,
to build massive weaponry to protect ourselves
from each other.
Don't you think instead we need some sort of valid reason
to live in nature's universe?
To really honour and protect our fellow-participants
the animals – their lands and territories,
as part of nature's miracle;
it's delicate balance
that pivotal interconnectedness
we alone could never make –
before it's too late?

Danny Gardner

Disconnect

Water courses over thousands of years
carves arteries across our country
emits a crucial pulsing rhythm.
Aquifers gulp the tropical downpours.
Rain soaks the earth, flows to be welcomed
in wetlands, lakes, oceans and along the way
evaporates, rides on the wind.

City dwellers are lulled into forgetfulness
immune as children, to a crisis unfolding.
They flounder under desultory drab raincoats
beguiled by rain that hammers down
rushes across their shrinking outdoors
morphs into storm water, drains into grills
gurgles with mystery and is thence no more.

Beyond the cities, human endeavour forsakes
stark outcomes. The fragility of our country
ignored, after generations of cultural reverence
asserts itself, covets a transfusion of insight.
Wild rivers no more. Bores splutter in despair.
Water, like blood, spills across our future.

Michael Keating

It's Only

It's only a bird
(jewelled flit of finch
speckled splash on air)
we need its habitat
to feed our herd.

It's only a tree
(ninety metres of *regnans*
five hundred years a king)
we need more pine plantations
surely you agree!

It's only a river
(brown, broken artery
serpentine and slow)
we must have irrigation
for our crops to deliver.

It's only a bit of ice
(ancient mass of glacier
in cracking, crevassing retreat)
to find oil beneath
would be nice.

It's only a planet.

Geoff Lucas

The Grey-headed Flying Fox

Pteropus poliocephalus

The extraordinary presence of things!
I awoke mid-dream to their blossomy gurgles
flexing sound between the tolerable and the outrageous,
a faint wild-animal smell wafting in the window;
bats bearing their own wisdom,
pushed incandescent towards extinction.
We are drawn together at the forest's receding tide,
cement and bricks are scabbing the land,
an army is advancing, going heavy,
forgetting the flowers.
Are we forgetting the vast, breathing element
in which we are corporeally embedded?
Are we afraid, or too arrogant,
to uncentre our thoughts from ourselves?
We must change our anthropocentric view
and listen to the earth chronicling our crimes against it.
It keeps me awake knowing everything
has its own magnitude, its wild integrity,
even the Hendra virus.
Among the robust and the threatened,
the illustrious and the humble,
everything is radical and radiant.

Cassandra O'Loughlin

Intergalactic Tourism

I.

close your eyes and imagine deep space
next picture a tiny blue planet orbiting a yellow star

now zoom in to the planet until you can see its moon
remember to dodge the dead satellites in the graveyard orbit

II.

you're in the cockpit of a space shuttle
program your controls to land on the moon
make sure your jet pack is working
and your helmet visor is coated with gold
to protect you from the sun's rays

step on to the surface and gaze at the footsteps
in the sharp shards of dust
marvel at all the incredible sights
two golf balls, a watch strap, nail clippers, towels,
shaving cream, twelve pairs of space boots, gloves,
used wet wipes, electrical cables, crashed probes,
a falcon feather, bags of vomit and six American flags

Indrani Perera

Advocating the Earth

Relentlessly protest
for earth made barren
by a scorching wind
upsweeping the detritus
of neglect and misuse,
reject the profit motive
no votive offering
to the gods of capitalism
creators of a schism
in the human spirit
while the true of voice
weeping for charity
are thinned
to a whisper in the wind.

'To have or to be',
a verity for all who see
past illusory needs
refusing lies – the seeds
of destruction,
for truth is ever thus
a now or never choice,
them or us.

Adrian Rogers

Backwater

Backwater: Hawkesbury River, NSW

Patonga is the last stop on a road winding in
from nowhere. My headlights scan the forest
closing in, as I take the descent to a bay ringed
with lighted cabins, a wide river open to the sea.
I hear fishermen calling over water. They wait
for an ebb tide, a low moon to set dragnets
in shallows across the bay, trawl for prawns
massing in sandy beds. Small and large caught
as they swim out to sea, the by-catch discarded
tossed to gulls circling on the early run home.

Currents slow, as I head up river. Oyster beds
staked on tidal mudflats are failing as the city
grows closer. Acids flow in run-off after rain,
threatening future life in the upper reaches.
I glide to a quiet backwater where mangroves
survive despite the brackish water. Each year
I find depleted shoals of blackfish waiting
for the summer tide to take them out to sea.
Past fishermen setting their nets wide, hoping
for a new catch to fill their shrinking quota.

Brenda Saunders

Haiku

soaring forest heat
burning bushes black ash flies
only spring – deaf ears

Garth Alperstein

…the affairs of men…

Julius Caesar, 4, iii

Above Hawaii, dazzling skies, clear and blue;
other islands, Kiribati, Tuvalu,
are sinking under rising tides.
Further west, a continent lies
engulfed by smoke.
Bush is burning, choking, west to east;
anger ignites the populace.
For decades, warned, they see it's too late now:
if only 'taken at the flood'…
Others claim 'it's just God's will.'
Meanwhile, animals who don't have words,
just stumble, scream and fall.

Last night I dreamed of kangaroos, paws burning,
tumbling into Canberra from the bush,
and scorched koalas struggling, drowning in the Lake.
And from the Hill, happy Messianic throngs
stamp and clap to 'All things bright and beautiful'.
Their song echoes to the coast
where seas lap higher up the shore,
everything out of season under heaven.
Time and tides turn while we watch the planet burn.

Janet Upcher

Ad Break

under the belfry
of the blinking eye
bats swam

holding a lump of coal
like holding Satan

flames
inferno holiday

a high-pitched
screech, Koalas make
when burnt

our prayers and thoughts
are with you, on
Hawaii sands

they want to be out there
scorched, breathing fine
ash particles

we'll return, after this
Ad break

Melinda Jane

The Front Moves Closer

The most potent media ever devised
– television, worried thoughts about a lover
and a diffident friend brought to enragement –
deliver images of punishing nature.

As fire blinds and maims,
a vacuum of political action howls,
multiplying as the blaze eats
the landscape,
emptiness deafening.

The media advisers spin inaction
into a tornado,
powering the 24-hour news cycle,
blowing it off course.

When even the wind succumbs to exhaustion,
we are left with an unearthly noiselessness,
– the silence of what's lost,
the soundless mouthing of platitudes
and my friend now quiet again,
hoarse from shouting.

Derek Baines

The Burning of the Great Statue

The statue loomed deathly dark,
sintered on the buttercup horizon.
Was it a figure of a man?
Or a black hole sucking light?
Or a lump of coal?
On closer inspection
it was deception, for coal at least burns bright.
The visionless eyes and unhearing ears coalesced and
the smooth mouth oozed voodoo prayers to some jesus
as flames flicked its flinty pockets.
This was no monument of proud, polished bronze,
but lead, sinker of dead fish, malleable, hollow plumbum,
glibly bubbling hot empty air
as it melted and catastrophised the cut lawn.
And all around it, along with our tomorrows,
the ants burned,
the bees burned,
the bugs burned,
the innocent and the soft hearted,
as the aching vapours rose and contorted,
distorted and scorched the very belly of heaven.

The News paper men came, flapping in the heat, breathlessly
capitalising the important I, their curling words blotting the
clean white paper lauding 'The Great Statue'.

Jane Carmody

Burning Times

I rant I rage I protest as the country burns in
great hellish conflagrations of roaring flames
billowing smoke swirling black, sky aflame
over this land, across the Tasman & around the globe.
Animals burn on the run; birds bats insects bees
and ancient trees tumble in the cremating air.
I rant, rage, protest as fire engines roll over & planes
& helicopters crash in explosive forces of burning air.
Incineration in fiery coffins of firefighters haunts,
their dying a living hell after year upon year
politicians turned their backs, eschewing the knowledge
that without the crucial clearings this country *would*
burn and burn and burn,
an Australian Armageddon *would* come.
It came and the country mourns and mourns.

How many are the leaders responsible for
the hubris of turning away, minds closed, averted,
choosing instead to stear the country toward dissension,
social upheaval, and a polity barely focused on
the welfare of the land and it's people? How many?
Inferno, fire, destruction of staggeringly vast swaths
of land all a modern Hadean reflection of ruthless hearts,
the ugliness of ruptured politics, and the silencing of
the voices of prophets.

Jocelyn Munro

A Prayer From the Inferno

I went out to the orange night sky
because Mother Nature's dying,
Smoke haze clogged my lungs
Politicians well-tanked in lies.
I saw the Four Horseman
summon up a fire thunderstorm,
embers spit miles out into the ocean,
heard innocents scream as gas bottles exploded,
I saw vibrant birds plummet to charcoal
beaches stacked with blackened torsos.
Billions of our marsupial companions have died
yet our so-called leaders continue their denial,
token gestures, dragged kicking from a Hawaiian holiday,
Why don't you stay away if you've nothing good to say?
Like Nero you're fiddling while the rest of us burn,
Our porcelain shields of ice are collapsing,
our oceans choke with swirling isles of consumer waste,
we need to get out of diesel monstrosities, blaring screens,
tell the money grubbers we're not listening to their greed.
Maybe she'll then return to stroke us on our peeling heads
and take us back to Eden's blue white realm of the blessed.

Mark Cornell

Lungs

In early 2020, Canberra's air quality was the worst in the world, due to smoke from bushfires in NSW.

You would not have thought
that the sky could be so heavy,
shrouding our shoulders in lead.
Needles stick in throats and eyes,
daggy masks are bought *en masse*.
Lungs are stuffed grey puddings
stirred and stirred, until air
is spooning itself inside.
Treacle-thick. Far from sweet.
You would like to release
some shouted statement,
fierce enough to pierce
the foul, complacent clouds.
But all you produce is a cough,
scratchy as a baked echidna.
That the sky could be so heavy –
who could, or should, have known?

PS Cottier

Cloudy Skies, No Rain

(December 2019)

Cleaving the waters surface with a shudder.
Knowledge hits home with a splash
That ripples of climate change begin quietly
Like the beat of a butterfly wing.

No rain falls from cloudy skies.
Raindrops mingle with smoke dust.
Cremated remains of Country.

Shadowing a blood red sun
Ash falls into blackened seas.
Milky Way, a memory.

Vast Gondwana. Ancient Land.
Mysterious Being. Violated.
Sacred places laid open.

Her children's screams grow silent.
Vanished into Dreamtime.
Nature's dried too deep to weep.
A funeral pyre to human greed.

A profusion of tears leave paltry, salty stains
On my parched and guilty skin.

Catharine Steinberg

In Silence

I can protest all I like but soon you won't be
here. Each time I visit there's a sign and today
your V-neck shirt reveals the bones in your chest
pressed close against your thin-stretched skin.
There's too much death and destruction now.

It's disappointing, is all you say of your feeble
muscles; with no strength in your bird-like legs,
none to raise you from your chair. You don't
'rage against the dying of the light'. As we sit,
fires storm through this land. When you listen,

it's with eyes alert for every nuance. When you
speak, it's with words honed well in silence. We
don't talk of the hectares of flames, the ashened
towns, the loss for the living, all the lives lost –
no, we won't. I let your silence envelope us.

Kathryn Fry

If...

If we could collect the CO_2 spouted by leaders,
some clouds of smoke would disperse.
If only the hand that gave
was bigger than the hand that kept taking
leaving the land naked.

If the incessant debating of climate change
was translated into steps,
could we walk down a path of hope
before the footings are eroded?
If tears held back by the stoic and the broken
were let to flow, we could refill empty dams.

If the world focused as one
and agreed that time is short,
but actions must be rapid,
we could start healing our earth,
clearing our moral mortgage
so futures may inherit
free flow of rivers and skies of sunlight
instead of ashes.

Bernadette Anderson

No fireworks

Cancel them.
Our skies roar, blood red,
thrust up orange plumes,
billow satanic blackness.
Not enough colour?
Too little clamour?
Not enough thrill of fear?

How dare any council, town, city
spend money on a fireworks display,
send thousands of dollars to pollute a sky,
already dust-filled, smoke-hazed?

Save it.
Give to hands desperately reaching out
from drought and fire.
May we know once more
a clear sky, lit by the purity of stars.

Dawn Colsey

A Kinder World

I want a kinder world of governments
that serve their people, not their power.
Avert dissent.
Economies in which the world can flower
and people breathe and live, not bow and cower

I want clean air, mutual prosperity
sustainability, with solar, wind
electricity
economy, ecology aligned
a balance between nature and mankind

I do not want to go on protest tours
declaring that my interests matter
more than yours
I do not want to coerce or flatter.
Just let forgiveness grow, revenge scatter.

We have a common problem, a mutual
concern; our climate breaking down.
Don't stay neutral;
more than protest, solutions must be found
to save ourselves upon this sacred ground.

Margaret Clark

The heat's on

Insistent as climate change deniers,
will these warm days never cease?
We sweat and wait
for the cool caress of autumn
which isn't even on the radar.

Impassive, Gaia valiantly turns on her axis
drifting through space,
waiting for a brighter species to evolve.
Our children nonchalantly tap at screens
in languid amusement as we worry, too late,
about the next disaster.

Are we really tempted
to pass the buck to the engineers
and their big nasty space toy solutions?
Aluminium flakes for breakfast, anyone?

No, lock the gate to the miners
and the doors on their masters
cosseted in boardrooms,
methane issuing from their foul mouths
as the earth burns.

Brendan Doyle

A Tree's Despair

When noxious vapours dance upon the air,
I don't despair; but persevere with life,
absorbing all the CO_2 I care,
and other gases causing endless strife.

When houses built of lifeless steel and brick
march up my hill and settle all around,
and selfish tenants shear my spreading sticks,
I don't despair, but bravely stand my ground.

When drought entwines its fingers: dries and thieves,
I don't despair, but slow my rate of growth
by closing the stomata in my leaves,
and readying myself to withstand both.

But I despair of rising global heat;
the fires fuelled will lead to my defeat.

Kristin Martin

Prometheus

Look at the maps! you said.
We are still dying.
And we didn't care to hear
or know how to stop it.

>We know many things
>with our science based on evidence.
>It does have a bit of trouble
>keeping up with our ravages.

Then all the animals burned.
And most of the plants
and houses
and some people.

>*Please!* we said. *Take over here.*
>*We can't do burning off*
>*in the old way*
>*that you know.*

By then the land was laid waste,
and we were past repeatable
punishment for stealing power,
or any human knowing.

Carolyn Masel

Choking

for decades experts had called for action
warned of disaster   their words futile   rain

on stone gardens   politicians knew best
praised silence   their jest merited no place

in months of inferno   they spurned firies
pleas for help   made no   plans for crisis

flames roared from tree to tree   blackened earth
kangaroo and koala roasted alive   dying screams

shiver   limbs and leaves ablaze   crash   sparks
ignited grass   broken bricks   twisted metal   fighters'

eyes red-rimmed   faces sooty   owners fled
beaches choked on toxic smoke   the longest

fire-season   in history was no mystery   heatwave
national park fuel build-up   politicians' porkies

and carbon credit deceits   the death clock ticks
fast faster   our voices must be heard
                    it's three seconds to midnight

Decima Wraxall

A Privileged Life

for Ella

I've lived a privileged life
Growing up in post-war England
Surrounded by unspoiled countryside
I came to Australia as a welcomed migrant
Have raised my children
In a society I believed free of bitter prejudices
Material possessions holding no allure
I focused on being 'brave enough to be different'
I refused to watch television or read newspapers
Even working in Centrelink for twenty-five years
Didn't really alert me to terrible injustices

Recently a beloved granddaughter wistfully said to me
'How am I gonna explain to my kids
About all these extinct animals?'
I was shocked into wakefulness
And that was before millions of creatures
Perished in catastrophic bushfires

I, who have had such a rich and fulfilled life
Find I am overwhelmed
So much to protest against
I don't know where to begin
I, like so many, am shamed

Brenda Eldridge

The Final Stand

for Greta Thunberg

How loftily they brushed aside
her passionate despair;
with the arrogance of empty pride,
the deniers didn't care.

As forests flame and rivers fall,
the seas begin to rise,
while disbelievers mock the call,
with disingenuous eyes.

She stood before this world alone,
and told of hope betrayed;
a generation cruelly thrown
upon the barricade.

How Dare You! is a final stand
against darkness and neglect;
the banner for a burning land,
with grace to resurrect.

Ian McFarlane

Industrial Revolution

Fossil fuels
Clothe the world
Seal the skies
Broil and scald
Droughts and storms
Fires and fumes
Coral and fish
Islands and trees

Rivers of coal
Glint and flash
You stand beside
mountains of cash
You would not know
You could not see
You move around
Unsteadily

The earth will dry
No juice will flow
you ask   you cry
what can we do
you ring your hands   repent   retract
fall to your knees   Too late for that…

Maureen Mendelowitz

Action to stop Climate Change! 'When do we want it? Now!'

on a dying planet
sharing wonder with small children
tracing the blue metallic sheen
of a black flower wasp under garden sun
and after rain rolling silver spheres
around nasturtium leaves

watching a caterpillar's colourful parade
across a green poem
we ask…who will you become?

'I've never seen a black swan'
lift from my page through open window
to bay where it bobs with mood of sky

we wonder about snails creating
silver art under stars,
caterpillars inside cocoons knowing
in darkness they're already beautiful

a gift of tiny feathers from small hands –
'the godwits will return soon'
…my hopeful heart takes flight

Robyn Cairns

Difficult Endeavours

The man who invented the wheel
started us on our inevitable steps
towards climatic confusion.
It went from Wow, we can do *this*, we can do *that*
to now, We *deserve* this, we should *have* that.

So who do we argue with today?
The money-making machines of massive
corporations and companies; corruption
in its duplicity?

I protest about global warming
but will anything change in time?
Materialism has come so fast
our knowledge of its effects can not keep up.

This government might reduce the local heat,
but it cannot compete with nations without conscience,
it cannot stop the unmitigated burning of
thousand-year-old rain forests that smoke out the sky
and upset the once dependable weather patterns

We are left with our own destiny of a
warming world racing through geological time.

Judi Hearn

the ashes of ignorance

we need to go back
to come forward
back to the people of our land
the ones who burned with years
of thousands
the undergrowth
for the knowing
to protect
tree canopies where
Bad Fellow Fire
lies await

indigenous hands
tied by settlers
slowly old ways
almost forgotten in
generation purification
white practices
now making
catastrophes unequalled
we need to go back
before the forward
is forever lost
in the ashes of ignorance

Myra King

Sonnet from the heart

The sonnet suits genocide. Ancestors
dodged arsenic in the flour to pass down laws
of Country to an old man whose vivid
dream kills off the last Mutitjulu kid,
her brain fried from petrol-sniffing. Elsewhere,
descendants thrive, become leaders and dare
to cure the toxic silence, clear the debt,
bring optimism to the last couplet.

The sonnet gives reconciliation.
Makarrata is the culmination
of the agenda; sing along to
a home-grown anthem called Uluru.
And imagine, imagine the weight
of an indigenous head of state.

Jack Oats

Black Stump

for Aunty Joy Robinson

Fire in the willows, &
the white man sprints to pumps;
the foxes and the rabbits split
& the conflagration jumps –
over sheep that sleep like pillows,
across the farms it shows no pity –
the orange sky is over-lit –
now hungry flames lick to the city.
I walked across the riverbed
where the platypus are penned;
where white man wrecked the watershed
moaning 'when will this drought end?'
At last it's White Australia's turn:
let's hope we blacken as we burn.

Tim Metcalf

Fly the Rag

Hoist the rag and let it fly
and burn its fraying tatters!
The stars drowning in a navy sea, isolated, white and girt
Seven sharp points ready to shred any
who would dare come near.

Look up! Do you still see it?
Its supremacy above even the very stars,
the spectre of a colonial past;
a flag made of flags upon flags
emblazoned on yet another flag.
This is not the image of the country I know.

Paint for me a sea of blood
pouring from the black bodies left by our genocides.
Paint the red soil of cleared land, now barren
below a blackened sky of carbon smoke,
and in the middle of it all paint for me the unblinking sun
which has seen our transgressions,
which will scorch our wretched hides,
which will crack our skin and wash the colour from everything.
Let its gaze fall on that old rag
and let it be bleached into a white surrender
or burned into a black oblivion
for it is of no country I have ever loved.

James Finlay

All Too Readily

Councillors with a mandate to govern East Gippsland,
you will be aware the Electoral Commission
has altered the title of McMillan – ever a swinging seat –
in response to a groundswell of grief, federal in its reach.
You should be all too painfully conscious in conscience
that you now sit stalled yourselves at a crossroad,
once you consult a map charting regional memorials
honouring a pioneer still renowned with naming rights
on street signs and monuments by rivers and lakes,
despite all too readily spilling blood onto water.
You will be acutely cognisant how much – worldwide –
voices passionate in their protest have pushed back hard
against a history of atrocity still atrophied in bronze.
Remember yourselves how a cairn on the Dargo Road –
beside a creek misnamed as Iguana, surely Goanna –
commemorates the spot where this Scotsman met his demise,
boasting his side whiskers and signature tam-o'-shanter,
only to see his cheekbone (its cast tarnished) meet a blow
from hammer onto punch – as hollow as a bullet hole –
having died penniless, despite all the tribal land he stole,
backed by his drover band of Caledonian horsemen,
a Highland brigade firing muskets as they charged
through families shucking shells at firesides by a creek;
leaving him to sample skulls as souvenirs in his saddlebags,
after all too readily spilling blood into water.

Rodney Williams

Illegal Becoming Legal

A large man from an oval office
declares that Indigenous lands
can be stolen by anyone,
'cos under might is right rules
diplomacy depends on thuggery
even if stunned onlookers recall
the rickety but important
scaffolding of international law
and are yearning for visions
different from the dogma
of Moses in a tightly buttoned suit
descending from White House lawns
with his amoral commandments,
so, take off the kid gloves,
speak the language of rights,
spell the letters of justice,
explain the routes to peace
and protest with Palestinians
that settlements are illegal.

Stuart Rees

29 November 2019, in response to US Secretary of State Mike Pompeo saying on 21 November that West Bank settlements are 'not inconsistent with international law'.

A Lament

Lay down your arms
bleat the peacemakers.
But children in war zones
have already lost theirs,
or their legs or their eyes.
They'll join a generation
of amputees soldiering on
with crude prosthetics,
if not pushed about in little carts,
or waving their white sticks,
sightless in the marketplace.
No teachers of braille for them
and signing help's unlikely
for those who cannot hear.
Look no further, though,
for possible participants
in games for the disabled.
Although it's hard to imagine
their homelands taking
an interest in paralympics.

Barbara Fisher

Collateral Damage

Syria 2017

Collateral damage:
aged five, not terrorist
but terrified
alone on a chair in a hospital hall
hair matted under
a cap of blood.

Collateral damage:
five months old, dust covered
but recovered
rushed to hospital by her saviour
together buried
beneath the bombed building.

Government and allies
rain death from
air-conditioned cockpits
while citizens starve and die
and innocents pay the cost
for all that is lost.

Dianne Kennedy

Hitchhiker

I see distressing TV images of wretched refugees
beating at the closed gates, that hostile barricade –
no longer welcome in the USA, not safe in Venezuela,
desperate, fleeing north from the despot's rule –
this mass exodus doomed to rejection.

I read of the annual migration south of monarch butterflies
escaping from the chill of the northern American autumn.
The newspaper tells of how a lone ranger butterfly,
compelled by instinct, flaps flimsy wings in a fickle wind
drops still fluttering orange, black and white
onto the path of a sharp-eyed cyclist.
At home, she gently tends the crippled monarch,
repairs its damaged wing, persuades an amiable
southbound trucker to take this fragile passenger
on the long odyssey to warm Florida…freed and flapping
both wings the lone ranger heads further south,
seeking the critical mass of seasonal immigrants.

Today on screen I see more confronting images –
resigned, sad and far too skinny people massing
together in borderline camps in their thousands,
refugees from war zones grounded, doomed,
no fight or flight left, hope in scant supply.

Sue Cook

No one cares

A long time ago, at the time of my birth,
They slapped me, and slapped me hard.
I protested loudly, but no one cared.

As I grew up, with scolding and nagging,
I protested, but silently, and with all my heart.
No one heard me, and no one cared.

Then I grew up and grew older, became a man,
Saw what had happened and changed my ways.
Adapted, accepted and tried to fit in.

Now I am old, and now I don't care.
I protest here and I protest there.
With croaky voice I have a go at many things:
The government, the way they treat some humans,
The politicians, the way they spin and lie and rort,
The council, the way my suburb is being neglected,
The neighbours even, and their bird-killing cat.

But does anybody notice? Does anybody care?

Margitta Acker

Too Many Birthdays

I've said it till I'm incandescent,
I don't want your workaday world
of mediocre stand-at-attention rulebook
return obligation
present!
I don't want
your spinning rituals of calculation,
your prayer wheel
of greatest show for the least expense,
I don't want your say-so on my life,
your emoji of approval,
nor care about the milliamp
of tiny thought you've exhausted!
So spend your cash on anyone deserving,
the CFS, Flying Doctors, Amnesty,
Greenpeace, Friends of the Earth,
Animal Welfare, Red Cross, Save the Children,
anything,
the whole dying world,
rather than pile on me the landfill
of your present
and I'll keep saying it
till I'm incandescent!

Gordon McPherson

The Unread File

Seething anger, red short fuse,
Hot blood pressure, blue black hues,
Disbelief and total shock,
Betrayed by those that should take stock.
They'd acted like a common thief
As they imposed their own belief.
They'd raced in anxious and prepared
They had a life they wanted spared
They coaxed, worked hard, each played their part
Shooting atropine into the worn-out heart.
Pain and sadness, my conscious bled,
For the man alive there in the bed.
Silent screaming in my brain,
His angel rejected when he came.
He'd been there, done that, loved and lost –
At ninety-eight he knew the cost.
The forms said clearly, Please no fuss,
The legal file marked, No resus.

Sound of mind he'd made his choice,
Not reading the file, they'd ignored his voice.

Marilyn Revill

Unbalanced

1.

The ageing are a problem says the politician
keeping them alive is a very great expense
of course there's a solution but it's quite unthinkable
though it would give our surplus a very welcome boost.

2.

My friend believes
every person has a guardian angel
I admit my arrogance
as I wonder how one so clever
can be so easily deceived.
However in my beloved golden ash
(which almost makes me believe in God)
there is a visiting bird
whose voice encourages me
to veer towards this notion.

As I teeter down the few steps
leading from deck to garden
it pleads in its avian voice
'be careful, be careful'
I AM being careful I reply
yet it persists
as if it really cares.

Betty McKenzie-Tubb

Ars Gratia Artis

I had a dream last night. I was federal Minister for
the new Mega-Department of Infrastructure, Transport,
Regional Development and Communications. Ushered
into the Cabinet Room, we were told to take our seats.
But before I could find mine, amplified music
started pouring from speakers – sort of gospel-style,
accompanied by hand-clapping. Each time it stopped,
we rushed to find seats but like a game of musical chairs,
one would be left standing. I thought I'd be fine, I mean,
I had four seats to play with. On and on it went, people
in and out, until finally there was only me, standing alone
before the PM. *Bad luck cobber*, he said, *forgot to mention
I gave you ARTS too but they couldn't fit it on the letter-
head.* When I went to leave he called me back, adding,
*Don't worry mate, you'll walk it in. Just treat 'em the same
as our ABC* and grinned as he slid a finger over his throat.

Gillian Telford

On 5 December 2019, Australian federal ministry reallocations
announced with departmental changes effective from 1 February
2020.

Give Me Olive Trees

It's been one hundred years since Renoir died
Painting and sculpting until his death day
Fingers gnarled as his ancient olive twigs
But eyes still bright to rounded arm and cheek

Now his hillside home is a museum
But the lush gardens too are his bequeath
Tiers of citrus – orange, lemon, lime –
And an olive grove of majestic age

Rescued from a fate as polished napkin rings
By his timely move to soft southern France
Their giant trunks and silver smoky leaves
In silent flutes of light thus standing still

Hence this artist of the sensual world
Saved an orchard from avaricious minds
Who notice only profit to be gained
Instead of the rich gift of gentle light
Of olive trees and art.

Tracey-Anne Forbes

I will not be cremated!

I will not deny my fellow creatures,
animal or plant
their use of this flesh,
built up from decades of consumption.
It's their turn now.

Gone, for most of us,
the wolves, lions, bears,
rejuvenating humankind,
removing the slow, the old, the sick.

Is there life after death?
Of course. We live on
as tiny creatures, plants, fungi.
Food for further levels down the chain.

When my life ends
it's me that ends, not life.
Now every molecule
of what I used to know as me
is part of another life.

Tell me, is there a greater miracle?
Life itself is everlasting.
Death, simply a transition.

David Harris

Small town

a teenaged girl has suicided on the railway track

the father thinks she did it to get attention
the grandmother had knowledge, but kept silent
the mother, a child herself, worried too little

too late the community meets to share sorrow and regret
the high school principal knows not how to proceed
some experts say it's better not to voice the word

while more kids act out their secret pain
and Facebook becomes a forum for their desperation
witnesses are hollow with disbelief

and psychiatrists, who thought they had the answers, weep.

Pip Griffin

The Question

The slave asked
What must I do to be free?

Many where aghast
At the questions audacity.

Some spoke of economic ruin.
Others predicted the end of civilisation.

Then from within of the crowd
A lone, clear, voice of wisdom spoke.

To be free you must first learn
To use the words of freedom.

You must declare freedom
As a birthright for all peoples.

Then challenge others to take it away
And you will be free.

Ken Setter

Free Speech?

Their words inspire bad ways, not good,
I wish to clench my ears to keep them out –
they sicken me, why listen? I know I should
cleanse my skin of them, scream and shout!
Though my pores refuse to let them in,
still the hate invades my conflicted self.
To listen, to hear their filth, is it sin?
I'm complicit – ghoul, not goodly elf,
for though I rightly say I don't agree,
what I do is clearly not enough –
the price we pay for democracy,
to be invaded by this vile stuff.
Unworthy lies portrayed as honesty –
the price we pay for speech is far from free.

Carolyn Cordon

A bull's eye view

I am the lone bull, there's a party of cows over the fence
I can smell their fragrance; each tail-flick fans my passion.

But I must stand, back to the wind in putrid mud,
while plush paddocks spread before me. What crime mine?

The little man in blue pants prances by most days, checks
my square pond, drops a block of old grass for me to chew.

Not a word from his skinny head unless I stroll over,
then a string of ugly noises and a raised rake say, Stay back.

I know how it feels to be jabbed. He sits in a rolling rock,
that roars like a sick cow and sends smoke from its rear.

One day I'll push the gate and his puny body into the filth,
kick him and his stick and take my herd to the hills.

Jude Aquilina

I Remember It Well

The first protest I ever organised was
for Animal Liberation, way back in 1982,
for the hens at Kuitpo Rehabilitation Farm –
rehab for alcoholic men, non-rehab for hens,
once free ranging, now crushed white feathers
caged within metal bars in large sheds,
while the Maughan Church – owner of Kuitpo – was still
marketing the eggs as 'free range'.

One Friday, busy market day,
we gathered in silence on the footpath,
Franklin Street, outside the church:
in the foyer the offensive egg sales took place.
Naive buyers looked surprised and shocked at our placards
with photos of the hens' pitiful plight,
while the minister and some hench men railed against us –
for their lost profits.
Not a skerrick of Christlike compassion.

We stirred with simple truth.

Alice Shore

Papercuts

Papercut on my tongue, the metallic taste of bro-
                                       ken
                                       words
in my mouth.
The violence in this house is flowering.
Not the purple violets of hurt bodies, but
the spreading yellow-green-blue-black bruises
of hurt words.

I write a letter to my pain, place it
in an envelope to post back to myself
to read in 10 years' time. As I lick the
envelope shut I cut my tongue
on the glutinous edge, bitter gum
sticks like the spit of a lover's kiss
to my parched lips –

Oh madness & pain how you once were my friend!
The friend of Frida, Joni, Plath, Love, all their
daughters & sons (who died, were given away,
& survived) – tore the hinges off farmhouse doors.

Spit mixes in my mouth with the blowtorched edge
of burnt blood. One taste & I know I am done
speaking to you through papercuts & violet words.

Natalie D-Napoleon

From the shadows of Weston Street

Ruth hid in shadows
her voice bruised by fear.
Daily he stole her words
letting them dissolve
before they touched the air.
Her Weston Street home, the edge
of her world, was sealed from within.
She tried to mouth 'no',
resistance rising as new life
breathed inside her.

The birth of Grace lit a spark
and Ruth's voice escaped
from silence. At first she scattered
fragments at him – till her words
became arrows shattering his grip.
She had been inside fear
for too long, she now marched
through it.

Once the locks were removed
Ruth taught Grace to write
the pages of her own story
with words that could never
be erased.

Joan Fenney

Legalities

Bridal attire and tapestried lace
walk down the street in a state of trust
soon to be torn and defiled.

Defence with its arrogant gown of black
cladding its torso in silken slack
posturing wig on its head,
proudly proclaims the innocence there
of delinquent impudent glare.
Oh legal, respectable, merciless crack
hold your head high as the cameras track
your progress into the court and back
your swagger down the street.

Belittle, befuddle, bemuse and beguile –
all your grand verbiage held there on file
accurate history marred.
But the innocent who suffered the pain
under the merciless battering refrain,
go from the court with nothing to gain,
offence by legality barred.
Speak not of justice, of wrong or of right;
when power, or glory and justified might
leaves self-seeking rapists walk free in the night
then mercy has finally died.

Anne Landers

Molestation

I feel his eyes, I feel his hands,
a myriad grains of shifting sands.
My flesh is pawed, my skin is clawed,
my private world meets his demands.

And so the flowers of my world
allow my eyes through mist unfurled
to see a better place for me,
a better place where I am free.

For here the air is calm and soft,
high up in my fantasy loft.
I'm safe within my crystal ball
where no hands fondle me at all.

Now it's our turn to expose
those hands that rip off all our clothes;
those dirty minds that perv and peer
and warn 'Don't tell anyone, my dear.'

It happened to you, it happened to me,
it happened to every one in three.
but that's not how it has to stay.
Molestation is not OK.

Margo Poirier

Home Sweet Home

When she'd escaped the daily kitchen grind,
The handwringing laundry, the ashen hearth,
The involuntary fertile factory line...
Inevitably in the aftermath
She demanded a vote, equal pay, due respect
But when she explained that of course this meant
Not *any* kind of harassment,
He cried out loud, 'The lady doth protest too much!'

Methinks Atwood's view has a pertinent touch;
Man is afraid he'll be laughed at.
Woman is afraid she'll be killed.
(On average, one woman per week,
is the current statistical DV drill.)

Small acts, dismissed, enforce attitude.
Small acts dismissed allow bigger ones through.
Frightening to speak out all alone,
Rather implode than be publicly stoned.

Then jungle drums from bruised walls thudded through
Sisterhood calling out brave and true
Silenced alone, but ever so much harder to do
When one by one, a collective drum,
Beat the rhythmic chorus cry of Me Too.

Melissa Bruce

No Game

Men shame. Women blame. It's a game, or is it?

When a man comes home drunk as a skunk,
hits his wife, leaves bruises, no game, but rape.

When a woman cries harassment
when her male friend defends his point of view,
that's no game, but rape.

Men shame. Women blame. It's a game. Is it?

When a woman tongue barbs her husband
over time, that's serial rape.

When a man puts down a woman
as being less than, that's serial rape.

Men shame. Women blame. It's a game. Think again.

Rape is never a game but an inhumane affront
to all of us, be we female, male
or in between. No game!

Martin Christmas

A Lovers' Protest

Why did you have to cut me the way you did?
With paper
And short meaningless words
Scribbled in blue ink which is always
Weaker than black, but not as brazen or careless as red.

Why did you not come and reject me softly?
Is it because your personality is the same name as a flower?
The handsome face that stares back at you from the mirror
Never asks anything of you except your utter admiration,
To the exclusion of all others.

Why did you say our differences were in 'sharp relief'?
Surely, this is more a term for geography or geology
To describe the landscape view of an outcrop of granite
Against the backdrop of a hot summer sunset
Than for a love distorted.

But the face in your mirror will comfort you endlessly
And love you always, without dissent, never asking why.

Mary Pomfret

No Codpieces at the Team Building Meeting

New Boss stops the afternoon
to tell us the score,
he's into cricket,
what a bore.

Roving eyes
tell us every day,
he's into breasts –
in a big way.

Bloke talk:
he has a dream.
Scrum talk:
gunna build a team.

He dreams testosterone.
I dream Toblerone.

But I'm not wearing boxers
not sweating near lockers
and please minute this –

I'll not be needing a codpiece.

Gina Mercer

Women Are Reclaiming Our Lives

Women are reclaiming our nights
Stolen by perpetrators of sexual violence
Robbed by emotional abuse and threats of poverty
We imagine not having to fight for our lives
Not having to train our bodies, hearts and minds
In daily self-defence and constant vigilance
We should be safe in every space we occupy!
Women are reclaiming our rights
To physical, psychological and financial freedom
We imagine a world created for our wellbeing
We celebrate our strength and resilience
We imagine words we finally breathe unafraid
Shattering the power of domestic silence
Every time that we speak our truth without shame.

Women are reclaiming our voices
We march with megaphones on main streets
Chanting women's rights! Playing rebellious drum beats
'Reclaim the Night' began in Leeds,1977
Women around the world still hold this vision.
We gather globally to protest and advocate
We demand that legal systems protect victims
We demand that 'NO' is respected as 'NO'
We demand that women's bodies remain unharmed
Whatever we wear! Wherever we go!

Gabrielle Journey Jones

Women who dare

This one chained herself to railings.
This one flew under the radar like a bird.
This one hid from a tyrannical regime
and wrote about her ordeal in a famous journal.
This one moved to the front of the bus
and changed the colour of protest.

All of them and more dared
to challenge the status quo
sacrificed themselves for change.

And today?
Young women are daring
united like never before
marching in red dresses
brandishing umbrellas.

One so young   still at school
confronts those men who rule.

Listen! The lungs of the world
wheeze and rasp. Enough!
I join the women who dare.

Avril Bradley

Commercial-in-confidence

Mr Relaxed and Comfortable jockeys
on the radio with Mr Shock and Awe

Jack and Jill climbed up the hill

their rants dog the air-waves
barking advice on the business of living:

to fetch a pail of water

acquire a standard spouse, grow your investments
preen your portfolio, fly the flag,

Jack fell down and broke his crown

seize opportunity, minimise risk
ignore the cost of compliance

and Jill came tumbling after

the mutual obligation
is to get it Right.

Anne Collins

Protest Poets in Prison

may we learn to love as effortlessly
as light falling into sea

may we walk in goodness
breathe in hope, breathe out kindness
a force for change, for all that lives
upon earth, the air and sea

may we fall into 'oneness'
may truth-seekers be heroes once again
generating energy and passion
for every soul seeking a dream

protest hatred, protest division
protest war and poets in prison
protest hunger, protest poisoned land
keep on protesting until we understand

how to love each other as effortlessly
as light falling into sea

Thérèse Corfiatis

What Goes Around…

The seventies was my decade of protest
Subverting the military industrial complex
We put a spanner in the means of production
Made the bosses shiver in their oxfords

Fuelled by outrage
One with the workers
We shared a universal ethic
And a universal spliff

Solidarity our watchword
In our songs
Our marches
Shouting defiance in the name of peace

Winning the peace non-violently
Which was our mistake
A universal ethic is no defence
Against rat cunning and money

And so the protest almost died
But faint embers remained
Fanned to a flame of outrage
By an environment that aches for it

Mark d'Arbon

Dissent

From all the scheming politicians' wares,
their oily words, their finger-pointing spleen
and rabid speeches made with pious airs,
keep us, the demonstrators, pure and clean.
Never let our upright moral fight
lend colour to their claims of spite and bile.
We will unite to chant with all our might
and march along in rows, or single file,
declaiming the rights of victims to the skies
in firm and trenchant voice with no respite
to others of like mind who tell no lies;
only we protesters see the Light.
Let us recite our mantras ceaselessly,
send those who disagree to Coventry.

Suzanne Edgar

I Will Protest

When you take my aged pension
calling it a welfare payment
denied to us dissenters
when we have to sell our house
to fund the doctors' bills
and rely on charity for food.

I will stand on street corners
with my harp and sheaf of poems
begging for attention
extolling what has passed –
when birds would fill my garden
of magpie chicks and possums
all I had to feed their young
and mist would wreathe the trees
rolling from the valley to the ridge.

I will sing of forest hollows
and creeks among the sandstone
tadpoles feeding on their mossy banks
when this beauty is a memory
I will not be silent
at the losses you have wrought.

Michele Fermanis-Winward

Best Protest

The best protest comes
surely by words alone
spoken, whispered, or shouted
in metaphorical tone

Remember 'I have a dream'
or 'How dare you' or
'May well might say, God saved the Queen'

So, morph your word
with heart and mind
rally your message in gentle chant
with contemplated lilt
rather than rant

Progress life's road of conversation
your word in thoughtful persuasion
not smash and break, demand and take
or disrupt, with seldom a pause
for surely then you will lose your cause

Roger Furphy

Stain

As I gaze upon the ancient city,
its history exposed through
derelict buildings
crumbled ruins
unstable monuments,

my eye
shifts,
scowls at
that solitary smudge
that silent, modern-day protest.

As I fix on
that flaw
on a façade thousands of years old,
that blot
on a scene reminiscent of eras gone by,
that blemish
on a vista unheeded by the impoverished,
I can't decide if
that single smear

capitalism sucks

has cheered or saddened me.

Virgil Goncalves

Suspense

I can cry and swear and loathe
feel shame   blame   guilt
I can give   open   offer
be still   quiet   write

Libby Goodsir

Defiance

Held tight in my phalanx
shield and baton ready
I face the city barricade
shouts echo from glass towers.

The chanting crowd carpets the boulevard
waving loud banners.
A bearded young man steps up
fist upraised, shouting defiance.

I hear the sergeant bark
He's the one, bring him in.
In vee formation we surge forward
truncheons flailing, we pin his arms

drag him, bruised, to our van
door slammed shut.
My private thoughts intrude
Is his courage greater than ours?

We are many, he is one
are others, like him, roving the street?
My fleeting vision, our prisoner,
on a beribboned dais, orating as President.

Geoff Graetz

Credo

I believe, as does Ivan in
The Brothers Karamazov, where
For him as long as there's just one

Person starving the ticket to
The club of the fed's priced too high.
Since as a member I've lived shamed

At having done nothing to help,
Able only to try and tame
Insistent demons of despair,

Depression, distress, disgust at
Belonging to humankind by
Reclusiveness, self-gaoling seen

As the equivalent of death,
As condign punishment for what
Part I play in the murder done,

This poem as a creative act
Of protest and dissent from life
A bid to soar beyond through art.

Graeme Hetherington

a poem with needles in it

a woman is arrested
for sitting and knitting in a chair
outside the door of parliament.
an absence of anger
just yarns from a sheep's back
and a chair built for restraint
and quiet activity.
click of needles click click.
the politics of days.
the clock resists any need to slow down.
click click
the wool tells its story
which is of warmth and giving
of making a future
and of the need to correct tension.
'if we need to protest extinction
why not do it sitting down?'
one knitting woman says
as she smiles at those dressed in red
and resists the orders of those in blue.
so, they arrest a woman for knitting.
the news reports that she is in good spirits.

Helga Jermy

Haiku

bush bird song
a sudden silence
log lorry passing

protest platform
the twelve-foot-wide
tree stump

old friend
each day there for me
giant eucalypt

Judith E.P. Johnson

No need

No need to feel sorry for me in my chair.
My mind moves; dancing with words & ideas.

I watch clouds rolling, birds soaring, walkers pass by.
I see birds' nests, knots in trunks & tumescent seas.

I listen to crickets shrill down by the creek,
smell fresh-apple rain & musty dry gums.

I scrunch leaves, feel smooth moss on a rock,
squash peppercorns for their pungent scent.

I eat mangos, olives & dragon fruit, & wear
zany pants & wispy, spiked hair like a garden elf.

I grow daisies, mint & yellow honeysuckle
amid bugs & slaters & leafy riff-raff.

In coffee shops I hear music, the hum of chit-chat,
the spar of banter & the clatter of plates.

Some people feel sad at my splints & my chair
but I don't. I live.

Just whistle or wave or give a cheery thumbs up!

Jayne Linke

Things

There are things that I could whinge about
or get het up and shout.
But they are far too personal
to push into the world.

There are other things that make me mad
and deep inside they make me sad
I say, 'That's nice'; hold my tongue
smile; change the subject if I can.

So it's useless to complain.

There are things that I lament
too late to mend that rent.

It's useless to complain.

And then there is that other thing…

But it's useless to complain.

And another thing…

But…

Jean McArthur

One Sheep

Do you see that one sheep over there?
It moves apart from the rest of the flock,
Seeming to defy the common behaviour of sheep,
Seeming to weigh up the option to follow or not,
Entertaining the idea that there is another way.
Not succumbing to the rules of sheepish behaviour.
That one sheep just might choose another path,
Ending the mob mentality,
Rewriting the rules.

Colleen Moyne

Rage again

Lost long ago, hidden is our past rage.
Stop the war, save the planet, we bellowed.
Buried inside and gone from centre stage
Now aged, unheard, our chants have mellowed

Science screams a bleak future warning
As glaciers crack, recede and creep.
Ice chunks crash to waters warming
Raised oceans swallow islands deep.

Our once enamoured earth is crying
Out to heed the ruins clouded in mist
From wildfires, tempest, ice floes dying.
Act now, it pleads, fix rifts in our midst.

Soak the sun, harness waves. The wind turbine
Whispers a reverie when less was best.
In our nest we yearn for times sublime.
We breathe our fear, yet still dare to protest.

Far away emerges a votive voice
Demanding dissent, exude what's right
Enraged, ignite the fight, make the choice.
From deep silence we summon our might.

Liz Newton

The Seven (St)ages of Outrage

innocence damaged –
plumes of purple crayon cloud the horizon

vocal dissent, strident argument,
indignant generational clashes

university learning fuels
democratic sit-ins, poster placards
grammatical and erudite

baby pacifiers and crèches
a mixed agenda of gender politics and privilege
the state of our planet now much more personal

email / internet democracy
each online petition signed
a panacea for dull despair

greed and avarice
flood the pipelines of power
the fate of the world feels inevitable

knitting nanas blockade the house:
Can't believe we still have to protest this shit!

Julie Thorndyke

A question

Standing by the pyre
waiting for the binding cords
to tie you to the stake,
or mounting wooden steps
towards the hangman's rope,
eager faces avid with their hate,
or marching with the crowds
who faced the masked police,
their rifles raised, tear gas ready,
or standing in the dock,
the judge's black cap poised,
ready to be donned…

at that moment did you wonder
whether it was worth it?
Given your time over,
would your cry still blazon out,
defiantly,
I protest?

Valerie Volk

The Unconquered

Dance, the devil orders. Dance.
The leering fellow with a gun aims to humiliate
wants a laugh
wants to see this feeble creature fall.

I dance. He thinks for him.
Fool. I do this for myself.

On shaky legs, strength comes.
My feet move with ancient rhythms
away from the devil's habitat
the now of threadbare days
humbling submissions, splintering of hope

to a truth where beds are soft
sleep deep, soup thick
laughter kind, respect a given.

You watch, poor devil
satisfied I know my place.
You do not understand
my dance is a temple
to the moments of grace where hope is born.

Wendell Watt

Last rites

Where will my dust go?
Will it be covered by footprints
Slow across the life I owned?
I accept I have to go. I accept
I did not sway, swing or rhyme in time
With the regular schemes of life.
I forgot to sing in time
Now I am happy, almost impatient
To accept the inevitable.
What did I do?
The odd prayer or two
For a god, but never for a chairman.
I have kept my notes hidden in this cell
Maybe my guard will read them
After a bullet dots the end of my rebellion.

Luke Whitington

Elephants on surfboards

All those self-appointed Caesars
and Caesarissas with their extravagant
gestures, battle cries of half-truths,
inaccuracies: shouting down those
who dare dissent, exploiting us
with psychology, confusing our minds,
decrying all experts bar minorities
who justify their stance. They've blasted
themselves tone deaf to nuance,
the world view from their padded bubble
stripped to film noir. White noise washes
over us like perpetual surf. Whatever we say
overruled, disregarded, disrespected –
for they know best what's best for us.

We need to be elephants on surfboards,
thick-skinned, determined, riding
their furious waves right into the beach,
questioning, factual, convincing,
polite elephants, clever elephants,
showing them other worlds
until the more fair-minded listen
– and we can have a conversation.

Tony Steven Williams

Reclaiming the Square

A dozen technicolour stalls
hold a mini local festival
to passively claim the square.
Plants and homemade quilts, cakes and jams are sold.
Some stalls have been lured here from markets.

Fencing by developers has closed off half the square
driving out stores like the fish and chip shop
where our young family bought dinner after weekend church;
for a planned multi-storey building
big enough to shadow this well used public place.

Government is pro developer
if locals don't get so restless
they might trouble the ballot box.
Constant resistance was met with jibes
'they're crazy greenies'

but reduced the planned building enough
to leave some sunshine in the square.

Paul Williamson

Not Guilty

Brain burn
Electric shock
Raw nerves in hot ash
Melts my mind
Disconnected thoughts
Examination of mind
Chemical and physical restraint
An exorcism
Suffocating in a claustrophobic cell
Hosed down in a brick cubicle
Observed through a glass window
Clinical
Cold
Us and them
I reject the abuse
Refuse to accept
The diagnosis
My denial
Evidence of my insanity
Finality of compromise
I beg to belong
To be normal
To be sane

Jean Winter

Cosmic Eye

I remember my hometown in the country,
Parched and dry,
Then in full flood beneath menacing skies.
I wore my maroon school tunic faded to pink,
As my protest against school rules.
The school believed in ugly conformity.
As a child I believed in an 'Eye in the Sky',
Extolling us to be 'kind to animals and people.'
Decades later I travelled in parched India.
I saw an enormous Egyptian eye,
Emblazoned on a conical, golden temple,
Reminding us to be kind to all life on Earth.
Cataclysmic bushfires rage and devour.
Nature is rising up at mankind's casual indifference.
Tsunamis and floods abound.
Nature convulses in earthquakes and eruptions.
Our planet is in the throes of grief and anger.
We need to DARE TO BE DIFFERENT
To protect our Earth.

Adriana K Wood

The fall of Communism
('The Russians are coming')

Our Slovak guide Ondrej says that after the Wall's fall,
he'd travelled to work for six months in Seattle,
and met a businessman there who'd bought a statue of Lenin
as conversation piece to set up in his mansion's yard.
When he'd told Ondrej where he'd bought it from,
it was Ondrej's hometown of Poprad.
And when he took him to see it, Ondrej had wept.
Homesick from his months away, he'd been reminded
of his childhood games in the town square.
'I cried! – over a statue of *Lenin*!' he exclaims, still amazed.

Back in the Communist heyday, some town joker had painted
a track of red footprints traipsing from the statue
to a pub on the square's side; and hung a carry-bag
of empty beer bottles from Lenin's extended hand.
And when the statue had initially been pulled down,
it was dumped on town wasteland for a year.
Being made from copper, and hollow inside,
it absorbed heat through the day and was warm at night,
and a homeless person had slept in it for a while.

These days, Ondrej tells, the Russians are back:
cashed-up, and made welcome at the High Tatras resorts.
'Russians are good when they visit in *cars*,' he smiles,
'but not when they visit in *tanks*.'

Paul Cliff

Speaking of Borders

I cannot forget that country of borders,
the fortifications, walls within ramparts
housing the zoo, where animals languished
until airborne bombings performed 'liberation',
obliterating captives and cages: the elephants
rocking in hunger and sorrow, the seal
swimming laps in a small, toxic pool,
the tortoise flailing the air, on its back,
that we poked upright with a stick through the wire –
all the sad creatures, barely surviving, victims of those
also buried alive. That's how it was in the East, in the
eighties: people and beasts with no memory of freedom.
Where two regimes once met in a lake,
the forest was shaved, so that those
who would flee from one to the other –
foolhardy, desperate, dreaming of liberty –
shot in the back as they crossed
no-man's-land, would vanish as if they
had never breathed. When the war came,
internalised borders turned into drains
for the bloodletting spree.
'Peace' meant the reinstatement of checkpoints,
so that the bitterness might be contained,
so that the plum trees might blossom in different
languages from those of their neighbours.

Jena Woodhouse

Frangipani in Barbwire

Hidden bombs rained for years
Five hundred thousand ton
Forming vast crater valleys
        they ran for red hope
An unknown repressive regime
His deranged dogma deceived a nation
Families shattered monks sacrificed
Innocence shackled photographed tortured confessed
Most were slaving
All were starving
        intellect   peasant   child   soldier
Dissent crushed
Millions died   bereft of comfort   bereft of ceremony
Protected by those bombers *resident evil* escaped justice

Now butterflies flutter through killing fields
as unexhumed restless souls appear during monsoon
as kodachrome sunken eyes endure despair
as ten thousands skulls bare witness to unspeakable crimes
as requiem tears of anguish persist unquenchable
and my wanting protest remains lost in time

Donna Edwards

Dissent

5 June 1989

His white shirt looked luminous against the
brooding bulky blackness of aggression,
that faced the slim short form with arms lengthways
at each side, both hands, like two fists, clutching
white plastic bags bulging with food? Guns? Bombs?
He Stood like David facing Goliath.
The image deprives the viewer of the
noise of dissent: A cry for help. A sigh.
The world waits. The tanks sit stock still. Unmoved

Rose Helen Mitchell

Visitant

West Belfast on a Friday night, darkness and boarded-up
shop fronts; slow, oncoming, predatory lights passing
thankfully on; his hands light on the wheel letting the car
feel a way up the Falls Road, the trespass line I'd crossed;
militant martyrs on end-of-terrace walls; his Irish drawl
thick, harsh as the engine's idle as we pulled up to a pub:
'Don't speak. Don't even open your mouth; even your
breath has an accent. Nothing English in here.' I stood
amongst others, tight-woven as Irish knit, the shamrocked
drink-spilled carpet sticky as blood; a quiet visitant under
pictures of Provisionals, the Virgin, the naked Saviour.
By a rock face in Kakadu I stood under a 4,000-year-old
image of the creation, an earth-painted frieze of ancestors
and spirit gods forming out the world in its Dreamtime.
Who dreamt that I too would dwell amongst these dry
rocks, these wind-blown grasses, this shallow dirt?
'All our history in this land. More'n your history here.'
Nearby, a brute, unrepentant blasting for more foothold
sinned a plundered earth that would still take us all back.
I wanted to speak out, decry, declaim. But again I felt
like a false guest, crossed over into conscience again,
with my invader's elocution, a product of my own tongue.
So I stood ground and bowed my head, silent, grateful
for land I could still put my heel down on, then trod
softly away: my pious, dissenting, but irrevocable steps.

Philip Radmall

this city is gay and cool to me

do you remember when passers-by hissed and spat
at us in the mall and cat
calls followed us when we linked arms
looked into the faces of the boy gangs outside the bars
walked away laughing, high on the heat of revolution?
can you recall when we knew our bodies were the sacrifice,
being out and gay a high risk to the world's moral fibre?
remember, we celebrated equality in 2017 with new rainbow
number plates minted in the year of the plebiscite –
now this city is gay and cool to me, no cadastral map
acknowledges an ancient ownership
nor the nine shades of blue in the Brindabellas.
Painting a roundabout on a Braddon street in rainbows
is not just gay but seriously gay, do the interjectors who
think that's cool are maybe not so cool, have no memory
of my struggle, ignorant of my history, that they voted for
or against on my behalf…cool and gay is more
than swings and roundabouts, more than a going around
and coming around, a being around
your votes can send us back to the fists of our urgent
histories where we are at once at stake
where gay is serious, cool is compliance, and evil
is so banal we do not see it coming.

Sandra Renew

Note: Hannah Arendt on the banality of evil

'Some monks were born to smile'

Vulturesque:
Looking more like
The birds soon to feed on him.
Bowed,
Robe patched, stiff with grime,
Looks above razor wire
To tops of bulgy, bare hills.
Smiles through broken teeth.
'Bow your head, insolent reactionary!'
Shoved down.
Head bangs table
Arms wrenched behind back,
Wrists bound tighter.
'What is the Dalai Lama?'
Smiles: 'I am old.
I will die soon
Anyway.
Go home, Chinese.
We don't want you here.'

Atop hill
Vultures circle.
Soldiers descend
Sheathing knives.

Steve Tolbert

Into the fray with LBJ

Side by side we press our backs
                into the road's unfriendly surface
Both hands each hold
                that of a neighbouring stranger
For the time being not a stranger
                      but a fellow warrior
Lyndon Johnson's plane has landed
        his car headed this way
The back seat accommodates Johnson   his ego
        and sycophant Askin
Run over the bastards sets the tone
Police seize my ankles
        drag me groundwise to a van
My back bleeds   I lose a shoe
Nothing compared to a napalm bath
                      or a sniper's bullet
History marks down the Vietnam War
        Johnson's grim aim not to be the first
                      of his kind to lose a war
My back heals   a few proud scars remain
I buy new shoes   a new shirt
History says little about those who struggled but failed
        to dent the egotistical myopia of the powerful
Ours is the sad compensation of being right
        but futile in challenging the great wrong

Greg Tome

Of Birds and Poets

A bird who dies in flight falls vertical through cloud,
Small heart that beat a trillion beats grows tired,
Slender strength dissolves, wings falter, cease to glide
Plummets to the ground. A ragdoll cast aside.
But a strange thing happened. (My eyes I fear deceived),
The arms of earth extend, a great wanderer received.
Earth – many trillion tonnes to its bosom holds the tern
Who weighs a hundred grams. As a breeze will sway a fern,
Or rustle leaves on tree tops, as mist bejewels snowdrops,
As sparrow's fall, to this life's end, the call to us – attend.

A poet who dies respected, his words like silver rays
Is cherished and remembered and lights up all our days.
Liu Xiaobo died imprisoned and was cast into the sea,
They hoped he'd be forgotten, unloved, by you and me.
But a strange thing happened. The sea rejected lies
And from his ashes strewn a flock of birds now flies.
There's one in every tree and all corners of the land
Are by a canopy of silver singing spanned.
Liu Xiaobo's life is lost, him we all must mourn,
But as we read his poems his spirit is reborn.

He said the darkness one day will cease,
We'll wake to freedom's songs of peace.

Maurice Whelan

rock-a-bye baby

soothed   cocooned…we'll keep you safe
sleep   sleep to our lullaby
rock-a-bye baby
on the tree top

tinny-eared jingle…reassures
defying zephyr-whispered warnings
and when the wind blows
the cradle will rock

short term fixes…billions of dollars
if a child wakes   distract with distractions
for when the bough breaks
the cradle will fall

empty hands   helpless…species die
hear earth cry
and down will come baby
cradle and all

then silence…but maybe
from the silence
like green shoots from black stumps
will rise   poems of possibility.

Colleen Keating

Night of the Supermoon

The time is out of joint, as Prince Hamlet said,
and I certainly wasn't born to set it right.
A con man and bully becomes President.
The whole world trembles in anticipation.
An old poet dies. That part of the world (much smaller)
which is still literate and compassionate mourns.
The poet set it all to music years ago. 'Sail on,
oh mighty ship of state…' he intoned, ironically,
against a background of rattling snare drums.
We will need his irony in the years to come.
And yet, and yet… I can still walk out my front door
at two o'clock in the morning, my iPhone in my hand,
and photograph the moon, which glows above me
like the biggest, brightest spotlight you've ever seen,
a witness to love and truth, if not to justice.
No paternal ghost stalks the battlements tonight,
but the injunction remains: not revenge
but reversal, while we can, restoration
of the right, however (and by whomever)
that is to be achieved – preferably, without the tragedy.

Stephen Smithyman

The Passing of the Fly

I must protest the passing of the fly.
Whereas a failing button's not too bad,
a broken zipper leaves me high and dry,

my easy-going nature goes awry.
A sticking zip's a thing that makes me mad.
I must protest the passing of the fly.

My zip derails, my wife lets out a sigh,
my children get embarrassed for their dad.
A broken zipper leaves me high and dry.

Can't close the gap, no matter how I try;
fair maidens see me blush and think me sad;
I must protest the passing of the fly.

Those teeth that nip the skin have made me cry,
I should have kept my old pants. Wish I had;
a broken zipper leaves me high and dry.

Four buttons out of five, and I'll get by;
it's buttons every time for me, my lad.
I must protest the passing of the fly;
a broken zipper leaves me high and dry.

Tony Fawcus

The Apostrophe's Lament

I'm threatened with redundancy. My little inky stroke
for long the bane of writers, has now become a joke.
I'm a cornerstone of English, determining its sense,
yet teachers call me hard to teach and learning too intense.

I'm written where I shouldn't be, negating erudition.
Or, worse, my rightful role's ignored, a baffling omission.
You've only to go shopping to witness it yourself,
apple's, pear's, as plurals, upon the grocer's shelf.

When I'm left out, the meaning of a written text is skewed.
I determine an elision, possession, and the mood.
It's not allowed to criticise, to question and to frown
when what they do to 'simplify' is really 'dumbing down'.

Although misuse and ignorance of grammar is widespread
it's movements in technology that fill me full of dread.
Denied the punctuation but a message to enforce,
will we revert to hieroglyphs or runes or even morse?

In writing, the apostrophe can punctuate with grace.
Language is evolving, developing apace.
Evolution implies growth, but language use will shrink,
if screens and beeps and lasers can replace the pen and ink.

Maureen Mitson

Milk

Oh for a carton of milk fresh and real
but how do I choose – you can't taste or feel.
Full Cream sounds good – is this Dairy Complete?
If not, then what's missing – sounds scary but neat
and tempts us with what the others are lacking.
Are they just the same with different packing?
And what of Lite or Smarter White –
if we don't use that, are we less than bright?
Does Original mean the rest are fake?
Skimmer or Trim – are they the same make?
Farm Fresh – do cows live anywhere else?
Then what about the Country Fresh
as opposed to stale. Just how do we know?
Reduced Fat or No Fat, High Fat or Low
Puratone, Heart Active or this one – Take Care.
Of what, may I ask – is there danger here?
High Protein or Zymill – how can you tell?
Or Farmhouse Gold – is there Silver as well?
And this isn't the end – there's Coconut and Goat
Buttermilk and Almond – put that down your throat.
Please take us back to the plain Full Cream
and lessen the choice before I scream
down the aisles of shelf after shelf
before I do harm to the stores or myself.

Ros Schulz

www.ingramcontent.com/pod-product-compliance
Lightning Source LLC
Chambersburg PA
CBHW070910080526
44589CB00013B/1251